Primary Sources of the Abolitionist Movement

Slave Narratives and the Writings of Freedmen

Caitlyn Paley

Cavendish Square
New York

Published in 2016 by Cavendish Square Publishing, LLC
243 5th Avenue, Suite 136, New York, NY 10016
Copyright © 2016 by Cavendish Square Publishing, LLC

First Edition

CPSIA Compliance Information: Batch #WS15CSQ

All websites were available and accurate when this book was sent to press.

Library of Congress Cataloging-in-Publication Data

Paley, Caitlyn.
Slave narratives and the writings of freedmen / Caitlyn Paley.
pages cm. — (Primary sources of the abolitionist movement)
Includes bibliographical references and index.
ISBN 978-1-50260-524-5 (library bound) ISBN 978-1-50260-525-2 (ebook)
1. Slaves—United States—Biography—Juvenile literature. 2. Fugitive slaves—United States—
Biography—Juvenile literature. 3. African Americans—Biography—Juvenile literature.
4. Slaves' writings, American—Juvenile literature. I. Title.

E444.P35 2015
306.3'62092—dc23

2014049204

Editorial Director: David McNamara
Editor: Amy Hayes
Copy Editor: Cynthia Roby
Art Director: Jeffrey Talbot
Senior Designer: Amy Greenan
Senior Production Manager: Jennifer Ryder-Talbot
Production Editor: Renni Johnson
Photo Researcher: J8 Media

Printed in the United States of America

CONTENTS

The Hardships of Slaves

The first African slaves were brought to America in 1619. Slave traders kidnapped them from many African countries. These Africans spoke different languages and had different customs. Yet they all faced the same horrors of slavery. They were packed into slave ships. They became sick, were starved, and remained chained below deck for weeks or months during the journey across the Atlantic.

Slave traders started to bring more and more slaves to America. Many of these slaves ended up living in the South on **plantations**, or farms where they grew crops. The North and the South were very different. In the South, farmers grew cotton, tobacco, and rice. These crops were difficult to grow without a team of people. Often Southerners decided that owning more slaves was the best way to make more money from their crops. People who

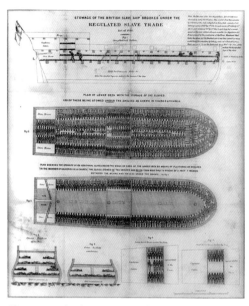

Slaves made their journey from Africa on ships like this one, often chained below deck.

owned slaves were called **slaveholders**.

Most Northerners weren't farmers. Northern slaveholders owned about one to three slaves each. These slaves were servants and laborers. Over time, the northern states began to outlaw slavery. **Abolitionists** campaigned to end slavery throughout the United States. Abolitionists were people who worked to end slavery because they believed it was wrong. Their name comes from the word "**abolish**." To abolish something means to end it, usually by passing a law.

Even though slavery was ending in the North, the South depended on slave labor. Southern slave owners were not about to give up slavery without a fight. They made up reasons to explain the need to own slaves. Here are some of the reasons they gave:

- They needed slaves to make money
- Slavery was good; the slaves had a job for life
- Africans were not smart enough to make their own decisions

As the North started to make slavery illegal, slaves began to escape to free states. They walked to freedom, hid on trains and boats, and at least one slave mailed himself to the North in a big box. Slaves had to be clever to get past **slave catchers,** who were people on the lookout for escaped slaves.

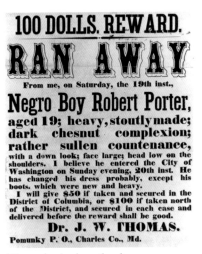

Wanted ads described runaway slaves and offered rewards for their capture.

There were rewards for captured slaves. Slave owners posted wanted ads in newspapers. This ad offers up to $100 for the return of a slave. In 1850, the **Fugitive Slave Act** was passed. A **fugitive** is someone who has committed a crime and is on the run. Attempting to escape slavery was a crime. This new law stated that former slaves living in the North could be returned to slavery. Anyone who helped an escaped slave could face jail time or fines.

In the time leading up to the Civil War, many escaped slaves told their stories. We call the books they published slave **narratives** because a narrative is a story with a beginning, middle, and end. Slave narratives were the story of a person being born a slave, their life as a slave, and escaping to freedom. These stories are full of pain and suffering, but slaves' escapes were often exciting and dangerous adventures. Abolitionists used these narratives to encourage others to protest slavery.

CHAPTER ONE

Slavery and Life on the Plantation

L ife on the plantation was full of hardship for slaves. They were called to the fields early each morning by a whistle or a horn. Planting and harvesting was hard on their bodies. Slaves knew they would work their whole lives without ever seeing the money they earned for their **masters**, which is what they called the men who owned them.

Family Life

Slave families were made up of a mother, father, and children. Husbands might live on a different plantation and travel to see their families on Sundays. Teenagers **courted**, or dated, one another. They got married when they became adults. Slaves had to ask their masters' permission to get married, even though their marriages were not recognized by the state. Sometimes masters

A few words or phrases used often throughout this book are "sometimes," "often," "usually," and "most of the time." It's difficult to talk about slavery without key words such as these. That's because every slave had a different experience. Slaves lived all over the North and South. Plantations grew different crops. Some masters were kinder to their slaves than others. It's important to remember that historians have a pretty good idea of what life was like during that time. Yet there are always stories of slaves that don't match the facts we find in history books. Olaudah Equiano is a great example. He wrote a famous slave narrative that was published in 1789. Olaudah's experience on a Southern plantation didn't last long. While he was in Virginia, he worked outside and in the **big house**. Then he was sold to his master's friend, who sent him to England as a gift for one of his friends. Olaudah spent his time in slavery sailing all over the world. He was a slave on Caribbean plantations and on different ships. This was a very unusual life for a Southern slave.

would sell a husband and force the wife to marry a new man. Masters wanted slave families to grow large. More people in the slave families meant more workers in the fields.

Slaves lived in cabins called **slave quarters** with their families. Sometimes a second or even third family shared the cabin, too. Usually up to seven people lived in one cabin. Slave quarters were small. Inside each cabin was a fireplace for cooking and open space for sleeping. Slaves slept on the floor, on blankets and straw, or on cushions.

Each slave had a unique experience during slavery. The slaves in this G. H. Houghton photograph from 1862 lived on a plantation in Virginia.

Groups of slave cabins were far enough from the big house—the house where the slave owner lived—that slaves had some privacy. When slaves weren't working, they caught up on chores around their homes and spent time with their families.

Slavery, from Childhood to Adulthood

Childhood was usually the happiest time in the life of a slave. In many slave narratives, former slaves say they didn't realize they were slaves for the first few years of their lives. This is something that Harriet Jacobs talks about in her book *Incidents in the Life of a Slave Girl, Written by Herself*. Jacobs writes, "I was born a slave; but I never knew it till six years of happy childhood had passed away." Many slaves remembered the fun and

Slave quarters were the simple cabins that families of slaves called home. Many people lived in a single cabin and slept on the floor each night.

games of their childhood. It was even common for slaves to play side-by-side with the white children who lived on the plantation. Though childhood was happier than adulthood, it was still filled with difficulties.

In James W. C. Pennington's slave narrative *The Fugitive Blacksmith*, he talks about his memories of being four years old. He says, "About this time, I began to feel another evil of slavery—I mean the want of parental care and attention. My parents were not able to give any attention to their children during the day. I often suffered much from *hunger* and other similar causes." Pennington's parents had other responsibilities on the plantation. They couldn't take care of their children while they were out in the fields, so slave children went hungry and played without anyone to watch over them.

Frederick Douglass also talks about being hungry in his famous slave narrative, *Narrative of the Life of Frederick Douglass*:

Our food was a coarse corn meal boiled. This was called mush. It was put into a large wooden tray or trough, and set down upon the ground. The children were then called, like so many pigs, and like so many pigs they would come and devour the mush; some with oyster-shells, others with pieces of shingle, some with naked hands, and none with spoons. He that ate fastest got most … few left the trough satisfied.

Here Douglass tells us that even when children got food, it didn't taste good and there wasn't always enough of it. He compares slave children to pigs to show us that his master didn't think slaves deserved to be treated as human beings. Masters gave slave parents the food their children ate. Each year, slave families got an allowance. They received clothes, bedding, and food. Slaves worked so hard in the fields that their clothes never lasted the full year. They mended their clothes as best as they could. Slave children often walked around half naked and without shoes.

Many children grew up on plantations. Children from the big house often played with slave children. Though big houses are often thought of as beautiful mansions like this one, most of the time big houses weren't very large at all.

Very few slaves went to school. Some slaves learned to read and write from white children, other slaves, or even their masters. Over time, the South passed laws making it illegal to educate a slave. There was a specific reason for this. A slave named David Walker had learned to write. In 1829, he published a book titled *An Appeal to the Colored Citizens of the World*. In it, Walker told slaves to rebel. Many slaveholders thought that reading and writing made it easy for slaves to spread "dangerous" ideas about freedom. Some of the first laws outlawing educating slaves were passed that same year.

Instead of going to school, some slave children learned special skills when they were rented to tradesmen. This happened to James W. C. Pennington. At the age of nine Pennington was hired out to a local stonemason who taught him how to be a stonemason, too. Adult men might also learn to be a blacksmith, carpenter, gardener, or other skilled worker. Slaves with special skills were usually rented to other blacksmiths or carpenters. The majority of slaves worked in the field their whole lives, though. They were in charge of planting and harvesting crops. They also took care of farm animals.

Any slave, skilled or unskilled, might be rented to another plantation. Many former slaves talked about enjoying leaving their plantation to work for someone else for a time. If a slave was rented to another plantation, he or she got the chance to meet new people and see more of the world. When slaves were rented to shops or nearby plantations, these assignments could last for any amount of time. A rented slave might fall in love with someone on his or her temporary plantation. If their masters agreed, they could get married. Then the husband would have to live apart from his wife.

Women did not get many chances to work outside of the fields. Sick or pregnant women, young children, and old women worked on "trash gangs." This meant they cleaned, sewed, and did light farming.

The Hardships of Slaves

Slaves were beaten, whipped, and abused in other ways. Masters punished their slaves for misbehaving. Sometimes they punished slaves just to prove they were in charge. This happened to the father of James W. C. Pennington. In *The Fugitive Blacksmith*, he writes that he saw his master whip his father after his father talked back. Their master said, "I will make you know that I am the master of your tongue as well as of your time." Pennington's master wanted to make sure that his slaves remembered he was in charge of every part of their lives. He could make rules about what to say or not to say, rules about what jobs slaves did, and rules about how slaves spent their free time.

One of the hardest parts of life as a slave was that they could be sold. Husbands were sold away from their wives, and brothers and sisters were separated at slave auctions. From time to time, babies were even sold away from their mothers. Sometimes family members were sold to a neighboring plantation, but most times slaves never saw their families again. Masters threatened their slaves that if they didn't behave, they would be sold to a plantation far away.

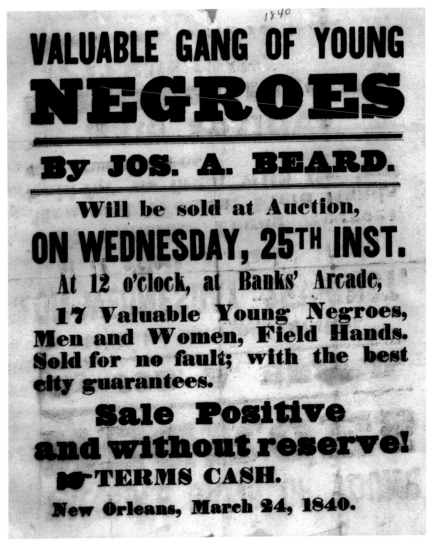

1840

VALUABLE GANG OF YOUNG
NEGROES

By JOS. A. BEARD.

Will be sold at Auction,

ON WEDNESDAY, 25TH INST.

At 12 o'clock, at Banks' Arcade,

17 Valuable Young Negroes, Men and Women, Field Hands. Sold for no fault; with the best city guarantees.

Sale Positive
and without reserve!

☞ TERMS CASH.

New Orleans, March 24, 1840.

Newspapers ran ads for slave auctions. Slave auctions separated families—after being sold, a slave might never see his or her family again.

Old women who were unable to work were sometimes given their freedom, but this was not out of kindness. Their masters did not want to feed, clothe, or house a slave who didn't make money for them. Generally, old men were able to work in the fields longer.

When a master died, his slaves were often sold to pay off debts. Otherwise, they were divided among the master's family members. For example, slaves might go to live on the master's brother's plantation. There was never a guarantee about where a slave was going to live or for how long. Many masters promised favorite slaves that they'd get their freedom when he died. It was a horrible betrayal if his promise was not kept or his family sold his slaves anyway.

Religion and Free Time on Sundays

Religion was important to many slaves. Most masters wanted their slaves to be Christians. Traveling preachers gave sermons to groups of slaves. Sometimes these sermons talked about serving God before serving their master. Masters didn't want their slaves to hear that, and made rules about what kind of church their slaves could attend.

Slaves experienced church in different ways. Some went to churches with white people. Some attended all-slave services with a white preacher. Others held their own secret church services where another slave acted as the preacher. Faith was a source of great comfort.

Most slaves didn't work on Sundays. They used their day off to grow vegetables in their own gardens, wash and mend their clothes, and spend a little bit of time with their families. Male slaves whose families lived on other plantations might get permission to visit. There were always strict instructions to return before the whistle blew calling them to the fields on Monday morning. Slaves who failed to return on time were punished harshly. James W. C. Pennington talks about these visits in his narrative.

Three or four of our farm hands had their wives and families on other plantations. In such cases, it is the custom in Maryland to allow the men to go on Saturday evening to see their families, stay over the Sabbath, and return on Monday morning, not later than 'half-an-hour by sun.' To overstay their time is a grave fault, for which, especially at busy seasons, they are punished.

Slaves often attended church on Sundays. Sometimes a fellow slave served as the preacher during secret church meetings.

From Pennington's description we know that the slaves could visit on the Sabbath, or Sunday, but needed to return to their plantations on Monday mornings "not later than 'half-an-hour by sun.'" This means that slaves had to be back thirty minutes after sunrise. He says that slaves are punished for breaking these rules. We've learned that slaves were usually whipped as a punishment. We can make an educated guess that Pennington is saying that slaves would be whipped for returning home late.

Slave Culture

Slaves developed their own culture. They blended ideas from all over Africa and from all over Southern

Slaves expressed their creativity in a variety of ways, including quilting. Slave quilts can be found in many museum collections today.

plantations. They told folktales and sang songs. Many African-American folktales are about tricking someone in power. Slaves knew they had to be clever to get a say in their lives. Slaves sometimes resisted their master without him knowing. From time to time slaves said they were sick, worked slowly, or made mistakes in their work on purpose. It was important to slaves to be able to make some decisions about their day-to-day life. Resistance gave slaves some of their power back.

Slaves expressed themselves through music, art, and writing. Slave narratives are an important part of literature. We can examine the lives of slaves through their words to learn what life was like during those years. Slave narratives were also a key part of the abolitionist movement. Even though slaves did not have much power in their everyday lives, their narratives show us what rich lives they led. There is power in their words.

Slave Narratives and Famous Writings by Slaves

Many different people wrote slave narratives—some were never even slaves. A slave narrative could be written by a slave who had found his or her way to freedom or by an abolitionist who listened to a slave's story and wrote it down for them. Like all narratives, these stories have a clear beginning, middle, and end. The beginning talks about being sold or born into slavery. Authors told their audience what slave life was like. The middle is usually about a successful escape to freedom in the North (or buying freedom), and the end discusses the experience of being free.

Escaping from the bonds of slavery was dangerous and filled with obstacles. Slaves had to think on their feet, endure great physical discomfort, and decide whom to trust on the road to freedom.

Escape

Audiences loved the escape stories in slave narratives. Many escape stories of slaves were similar to suspenseful fiction books that were popular in the 1800s. Narratives by escaped slaves William and Ellen Craft, and Henry "Box" Brown, for example, were big sellers. Their clever escape plans made exciting stories.

William and Ellen Craft were born into slavery in Georgia. Ellen Craft was the daughter of a female slave and her master. Because her skin was very light, it was easy to mistake her for a white person. Her husband, William, had dark skin. When they decided to escape in 1848, they kept their appearances in mind.

Ellen Craft's disguise as a slaveholder was convincing enough that she was able to escort her husband to freedom. The Crafts' cunning plan made them, as well as their slave narrative, famous.

They decided that Ellen would dress up like an old, sick man traveling with his slave. Women didn't travel by themselves in those days, so it was important that Ellen looked like a man. Ellen had to pretend to be sick in order to avoid conversations with other passengers on the trains and boats they took to freedom. There was another reason Ellen had to pretend to be sick, too. She couldn't write. Each hotel expected their guests to sign in. Ellen put her right hand in a sling. William placed a poultice, or medicine under a cloth, under her chin and tied it over her head. It looked as if Ellen had bad arthritis. The poultice hid the fact that Ellen had smooth skin around her jaw instead of a beard.

The Crafts' journey was not easy. An officer on a ship refused to sign their fake names on the list of passengers when they bought tickets. Another passenger stood up for them and the captain allowed them on board. Then they almost got stuck in the South at a train station. This is how William described the event:

They are particularly watchful at Baltimore to prevent slaves from escaping into Pennsylvania, which is a free State. After I had seen my master [Ellen] into one of the best carriages, and was just about to step into mine, an officer, a full-blooded Yankee of the lowest order, saw me. He came quickly up, and, tapping me on the shoulder, said in his unmistakable native twang, together with no little display of his authority, "Where are you going, boy?" "To Philadelphia, sir," I humbly replied. "Well, what are you going there for?" "I am traveling with my master, sir." "Well, I calculate you had better get him out; and be mighty quick about it, because the train will soon be starting. It is against my rules to let any man take a slave past here, unless he can satisfy them in the office that he has a right to take him along."

Slaves rarely traveled to the North with their masters because they might escape. Sometimes railroad workers or sailors checked to make sure African Americans had papers to prove that they were free. Other travelers might ask to see this kind of proof, hoping to catch an escaped slave and get a reward. William and Ellen Craft made it onto the train after other passengers were upset to see a sick old man treated poorly. The officer let them board the train to freedom.

The couple learned to write during their time in Philadelphia. Their narrative describes their exciting escape and includes stories of the hardships of slaves they knew, poems, and quotes from slavery laws. Their story makes it clear that the practice of slavery was not for the good of the slaves, even though that's what some masters claimed.

Like the Crafts', Henry "Box" Brown's slave narrative also tells an exciting escape story. Henry was born in Virginia in 1815. He lived on a plantation until his master, John Barrett, died. At that time, Brown's family members were divided among several other slave owners. Brown was separated from his whole family. He was only fifteen years old.

Brown went to live in Richmond, where he worked in a tobacco factory. "We were obliged to work fourteen hours a day in the summer, sixteen in the winter," he wrote in *Narrative of the Life of Henry Box Brown.*

Brown's life as a slave became too much to bear. His wife and children were sold away from him and were taken to North Carolina. Henry decided to escape to the North. He planned to seal himself into a shipping crate and mail himself to Philadelphia. Brown had a friend who was a shopkeeper. The man agreed to find a big box and to mail Brown in exchange for half of Brown's savings. Brown was ready to go.

> On the morning of the 29th day of March, 1849, I went into the box—having previously bored three gimlet holes opposite my face, for air, and provided myself with a bladder of water, both for the purpose of quenching my thirst and for wetting my face, should I

This print by Samuel Rowse shows Henry "Box" Brown emerging from his shipping crate in Philadelphia. Brown sold Rowse's art to raise money for abolitionist causes.

feel getting faint … Being thus equipped for the battle of liberty, my friends nailed down the lid and had me conveyed to the Express Office …

Brown spent twenty-seven hours in the shipping crate. He tumbled around, spent hours upside down, and faced rough handling—but he made it to Philadelphia and freedom. Henry "Box" Brown proved that many slaves were willing to risk their lives to escape. Brown could have died in the box. He wasn't sure he would make it to the North alive. Even the people who opened the box were scared. They were relieved to find he was okay. Stories such as Brown's have made a big point: many slaves would rather die than live in slavery.

Unusual Narratives

Not all slave narratives were written by former slaves who had escaped to the North. Moses Grandy's story is different from others because he did not escape from slavery. Grandy, born in 1786, bought his freedom, even though it took him three tries. Every time Grandy paid one of his owners the price they agreed on, the owner went back on his word. Over time, Grandy spent $1,850 trying to buy his freedom before his last owner finally kept his promise.

Moses Grandy was born in Camden County, North Carolina as a slave. He could not read or write, but he told his story to an abolitionist he met in England in 1842. His narrative is titled *Narrative of the Life of Moses Grandy, Late a Slave in the United States of America*. In his narrative, Grandy talks about saving up for years to buy his own freedom. He knew he couldn't trust his owners, but he kept trying.

After buying his freedom, Grandy made it his mission to buy his whole family's freedom. Many of their owners negotiated with Grandy. They asked for a lot of money because they knew Grandy really wanted to set his family members free. But finding his family members was an even bigger problem. About his experiences, Grandy wrote:

> I do not know where any of my other four children are, nor whether they be dead or alive. It will be very difficult to find them out: for the names of slaves are commonly changed with every change of master: they

usually bear the name of the master to whom they belong at the time: they have no family name of their own by which they can be traced. Through this circumstance, and their ignorance of reading and writing, to which they are compelled by law, all trace between parents and children, who are separated from them in childhood, is lost in a few years.

In this excerpt Grandy explains that a big obstacle in finding his children is that they did not share his last name. Every time one of his children changed masters, their last name changed, too. The fact that his family members did not know how to write also meant it was easy to lose track of where they were. Grandy points out that the laws that support slavery separate families, sometimes forever.

Though his children's names changed, Grandy had some luck tracking down two of his sons. He started by going to the first master they were sold to and moving from plantation to plantation until someone knew where they were. Grandy's narrative talks about purchasing the freedom of his wife, the two sons he found, and one of his grandchildren. Grandy wanted to sell his narrative to raise money to buy more of his family members.

Grandy gives us an important look at the way slaves achieved freedom legally.

Uncle Tom's Cabin is also different from other slave narratives: a woman who had never been a slave wrote it. Harriet Beecher Stowe was a white writer who had been born into a family of abolitionists. Stowe started to write

UNCLE TOM'S CABIN

UNCLE TOM & EVA·

Scholars consider Harriet Beecher Stowe's book to be one of the most lasting works of abolitionist writing. Stowe did careful research before writing *Uncle Tom's Cabin*.

her book soon after the Fugitive Slave Law was passed. She published *Uncle Tom's Cabin* in 1852. She felt it was important to tell others about the bad treatment of slaves. *Uncle Tom's Cabin* is a work of fiction, but Stowe based her book on true stories.

Uncle Tom's Cabin is about a master who sells two of his slaves, an old man named Uncle Tom and a five-year-old boy named Harry. Harry's mother takes him and runs away, but Uncle Tom stays on the plantation and is sold. In the end, Harry and his mother make it to Canada. Uncle Tom, however, is beaten to death by his overseer.

Life in the North

Even the men and women who had made the difficult journey to freedom weren't completely safe from slavery in the North. This was because of the Fugitive Slave Act, which stated that any escaped slave could be captured and sent back into slavery.

Harriet Jacobs experienced the effects of the law firsthand. She was born into slavery in Edenton, North Carolina in 1813. Jacobs ran away from her master and hid near the plantation. Some of her neighbors let her hide at their houses. Then she lived in her grandmother's crawlspace.

After hiding for almost seven years, Jacobs ran away to Brooklyn, New York. Her master never stopped looking for her, though. She moved to Boston, Massachusetts, and then Rochester, New York, hoping to remain free. When the Fugitive Slave Law was passed, her master's daughter came looking for Jacobs and Jacobs's daughter.

After escaping from her master, Harriet Jacobs hid in a crawl space for nearly seven years before making her way to the North. She wrote about her experiences in *Incidents in the Life of a Slave Girl*.

Here Jacobs describes the terror and pain the Fugitive Slave Law caused:

Many a wife discovered a secret she had never known before—that her husband was a fugitive, and must leave to insure his own safety. Worse still, many a husband discovered that his wife had fled from slavery years ago, and as "the child follows the condition of its mother," the children of his love were liable to be seized and carried into slavery. Every where, in those humble homes, there was consternation and anguish.

Harriet Jacobs shares a fact in this passage that appears in many slave narratives. When she talks about the "condition of its mother," she means slavery. If a woman was a slave, her children were automatically slaves. It did not matter if their father was her master. It did not matter if their father was a free man. According to the Fugitive Slave Act, children who were born free could be sold into slavery if their mother was an escaped slave. Harriet Jacobs's abolitionist friends bought and freed her and kept her daughter safe, too.

Some former slaves became famous abolitionists. Sojourner Truth is a great example. She was born a slave in 1797 in Rifton, New York. Her birth name was Isabella Baumfree, which she later changed to Sojourner Truth. As a slave, Truth was sold several times and separated from her husband. Her master made her marry a new man. Truth's children were then sold away from her.

Sojourner Truth worked hard to gain equal rights for both slaves and women.

Sojourner Truth finally escaped from her master in 1826. Afterwards, she devoted herself to helping others. Truth was a dedicated abolitionist and even lived with a group of other abolitionists on a farm for a time. She worked toward equal rights for women, too. Sojourner Truth became one of the most famous abolitionists, and is most well-known for her speech titled "Ain't I a Woman?" at the Women's Rights Convention in Akron, Ohio in 1851. She spoke from her heart and made clear points about the equality of women.

> That man over there says that women need to be helped into carriages, and lifted over ditches, and to have the best place everywhere. Nobody ever helps me into carriages, or over mud-puddles, or gives me any best place! And ain't I a woman?

Look at me! Look at my arm! I have ploughed and planted, and gathered into barns, and no man could head me! And ain't I a woman? I could work as much and eat as much as a man—when I could get it—and bear the lash as well! And ain't I a woman? I have borne thirteen children, and seen most all sold off to slavery, and when I cried out with my mother's grief, none but Jesus heard me! And ain't I a woman?

In this passage, Sojourner Truth points out that women are physically and mentally strong. She talks about being whipped, working in the fields, and losing her children. She reminds the audience that the treatment of slave women did not differ from that of slave men. She expresses her belief that women also deserved to be treated equally when they were free. Truth gave this speech because she thought that women's rights needed to be a big part of abolitionism. This speech confirms that former slaves helped shape the goals of abolitionism.

Slaves lived through horrible experiences that were rarely recorded. Authors of slave narratives made sure that people could read their side of the story. They wanted everyone to know that no one deserved to be a slave. Through their descriptions of their lives and their escapes, authors of slave narratives helped the abolitionist cause. Through their speeches, authors fought for what they believed in. They spoke for the slaves who could not write. They spoke for those silenced by fear.

CHAPTER THREE

Reactions and Consequences

Readers loved the excitement of slave narratives. The books were big sellers. Proslavery advocates, however, did not like the popularity of the writings. They knew that these stories threatened the **"peculiar institution,"** which was another name for slavery. Those who believed in slavery spoke out against slave narratives in various ways. They told their audiences the stories were lies, they targeted the authors of the books, and they wrote books and stories of their own that painted a very different picture of slavery.

Best Sellers and Targets

Slave narratives such as those of William and Ellen Craft, Henry "Box" Brown, and Frederick Douglass became a popular genre of literature. In the mid-1800s, many slave narratives were bestsellers. Harriet Beecher Stowe's *Uncle*

AMERICA

God bless you massa! you feed and clothe us. When we are sick you nurse us, and when too old to work, you provide for us!

These poor creatures are a sacred legacy from my ancestors and while a dollar is left me, nothing shall be spared to increase their comfort and happiness.

Proslavery propaganda, including anti-Tom literature, made slave owners appear kind and generous. They described slavery as a happy and comfortable way of life for slaves.

Tom's Cabin sold three hundred thousand copies the year it was published. This made it one of the biggest books of that time period. Stowe had worked hard to find someone to publish the book. Her publisher initially doubted it would be successful, so only five thousand copies were printed to start. Imagine everyone's surprise when all five thousand copies sold in two days!

Some people hated Stowe's book. Because of her writings, she was repeatedly threatened. Many people sent her angry letters in the mail. In these letters they wrote that *Uncle Tom's Cabin* wasn't true to life. Stowe's book even inspired a whole series of books in response. These books are called **anti-Tom literature**. In them, slaves are happy and love their masters.

Stowe decided to prove that her book was based on the lives of real people. She wrote another book titled *Key to Uncle Tom's Cabin* in 1854. In it, she included five hundred pages of careful research. Her friend Frederick

A KEY
to
UNCLE TOM'S CABIN;

PRESENTING THE ORIGINAL

FACTS AND DOCUMENTS

UPON WHICH THE STORY IS FOUNDED.

TOGETHER WITH

Corroborative Statements

VERIFYING

THE TRUTH OF THE WORK.

BY HARRIET BEECHER STOWE,
AUTHOR OF "UNCLE TOM'S CABIN."

BOSTON:
PUBLISHED BY JOHN P. JEWETT & CO.
CLEVELAND, OHIO:
JEWETT, PROCTOR & WORTHINGTON.
LONDON: LOW AND COMPANY.
1853.

A Key to Uncle Tom's Cabin proved that *Uncle Tom's Cabin* was based on true stories.

Douglass commented, "The most unwise thing which, perhaps, was ever done by slaveholders, in order to hide the ugly features of slavery, was the calling in question, and denying the truthfulness of *Uncle Tom's Cabin*."

Ellen Craft also had to stand up for herself. After the Crafts escaped to England, rumors began that Craft hated being free. She wrote to a newspaper called *The Anti-Slavery Advocate* to address these rumors.

> So I write these few lines merely to say that the statement is entirely unfounded, for I have never had the slightest inclination whatever of returning to bondage; and God forbid that I should ever be so false to liberty as to prefer slavery in its stead. In fact, since my escape from slavery, I have gotten much better in every respect than I could have possibly anticipated. Though, had it been to the contrary, my feelings in regard to this would have been just the same, for

Anti-Tom Literature

Anti-Tom literature was a popular genre, even in the North. There were about thirty anti-Tom books published in the 1800s. Proslavery advocates wrote these books to convince Northerners that slavery was good for slaves. The best-selling piece of anti-Tom literature was *Aunt Phillis's Cabin* by Mary Eastman. It was published in 1852. In it, Eastman paints a happy picture of slavery.

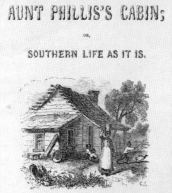

It was just sundown, but the servants were all at home after their day's work, and they too were enjoying the pleasant evening time. Some were seated at the door of their cabins, others lounging on the grass, all at ease, and without care. Many of their comfortable cabins had been recently whitewashed, and were adorned with little gardens in front; over the one nearest the house a muiltiflora rose was creeping in full bloom. Singularly musical voices were heard at intervals, singing snatches of songs, of a style in which the servants of the South especially delight …

Mary Eastman's book describes a caring master and slaves who rely on his wisdom. This is a common message in anti-Tom books.

Slave Narratives and the Writings of Freedmen

> I had much rather starve in England, a free woman, than be a slave for the best man that ever breathed upon the American continent.

Ellen Craft explains in this passage that the rumors are lies. She knows that life is terrible for slaves even when they have good masters.

Doubtful Stories?

Many authors of slave narratives were called liars. Others doubted that African Americans could write good books. Some critics said that mixed-race or "**mulatto**" authors were good writers only because they were partially white. James W. C. Pennington was often introduced as "having all-black ancestors" to prove them wrong. Pennington was a great writer. He showed that his abilities had nothing to do with the color of his skin. He helped convince people that there were other African-American writers like him.

Sadly, there was always the question of how well a former slave could write. It was easy to make this claim because many former slaves couldn't write at all. Many slave narratives were recorded by former slaves' friends. Proslavery advocates, however, liked to accuse white abolitionists of writing fake slave narratives just to make slavery look bad.

Many slave narratives included letters written by the author's white friends. The letters told readers the story was true. African-American authors needed these letters to be believed. Henry "Box" Brown's narrative opens with several letters. One of his friends, James McKim, writes:

I confess, if I had not myself been present at the opening of the box on its arrival, and had not witnessed with my own eyes, your resurrection from your living tomb, I should have been strongly disposed to question the truth of the story. As it was, however, seeing was believing, and believing was with me, at least, to be impressed with the diabolical character of American Slavery, and the obligation that rests upon every one to labour for its overthrow.

In this excerpt, McKim admits that Henry's story seems unbelievable. He knows that many people will think that Henry "Box" Brown is lying. McKim allowed his letter to be published so that others will know that Brown's story is true. McKim witnessed the opening of the box in which Brown had arrived and stood by his friend's story.

The titles of some slave narratives give us clues about how writers handled the doubts of others. For example, the full title of Harriet Jacobs's book is *Incidents in the Life of a Slave Girl, Written By Herself*. Sometimes slave narrative titles included "written by herself" or "written by himself." This was to say that the former slave wrote the book on his or her own. This helped silence criticisms before a reader even opened the book.

Unfortunately, Harriet Jacobs's book was still criticized. When Jacobs first tried to publish her book, she used a pen name, Linda Brent. This was done to protect Jacobs and her family. When people found out

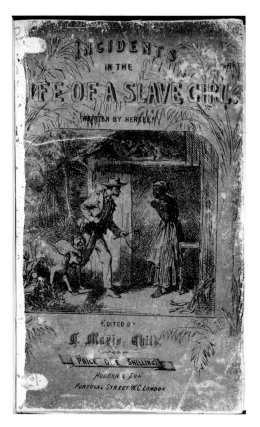

Harriet Jacobs faced criticism for publishing her book under the pen name Linda Brent.

that there was no Linda Brent, they began to doubt the truth of Jacobs's whole story. It was hard for them to believe that an escaped slave spent years hiding in a crawl space. Her story seemed too outrageous to be true. Finally, the fact that Jacobs's friend Lydia Child helped to edit the narrative made some people doubt that Jacobs wrote the book in the first place. Jacobs had to defend herself and her writing. Lydia Child helped. She was happy to tell others that she only edited Jacobs's work.

Another way Harriet Jacobs tried to defend her unpublished book was by teaming up with Harriet Beecher Stowe. Jacobs wanted Stowe to promote her book. However, the two ended up having a big disagreement. Stowe wanted to use Jacobs's stories as part of *Key to Uncle Tom's Cabin* instead. Jacobs felt betrayed by Stowe and never forgave her. It was difficult for Jacobs to publish her book without Stowe's support. She eventually found a publisher but did not sell many copies at first.

Her editor worked hard to promote *Incidents in the Life of a Slave Girl*.

One of the ways abolitionists promoted slave narratives was by writing reviews in abolitionist newspapers. In 1861, *The Anti-Slavery Bugle* reviewed *Incidents in the Life of a Slave Girl*.

> We have read this unpretending work with much pleasure. It is a veritable history of trials and sufferings to which a slave girl was subjected, but who finally triumphed over all discouragements, and obtained freedom for herself and her two children. The manuscript was revised by Mrs. Child, who is acquainted with the author, and who assures the reader that she "has not added anything to the incidents, or changed the import of her very pertinent remarks," the revision being merely for condensation and orderly arrangement. The style is simple and attractive—you feel less as though you were reading a book, than talking with the woman herself.

This review and other reviews in abolitionist newspapers helped Jacobs finally sell copies of her book.

Disagreements between Abolitionists

Some authors made their narratives a part of their everyday lives. Henry "Box" Brown, for example, started to go by the nickname "Box" after he made it to the North. But even some abolitionists disliked Brown's marketing. Frederick Douglass openly criticized Brown. Douglass thought that Brown shouldn't have made money by telling the details of his escape. Douglass believed that Brown stopped other slaves from mailing themselves to freedom. Once Brown published his narrative, slave catchers and postal workers were on the lookout for other runaways attempting to use the same method of escape.

Not all abolitionist authors agreed on the right way to fight slavery, either. In fact, there were arguments between different groups of abolitionists. Sometimes black abolitionists were **segregated**, or separated, from white abolitionists at meetings. They had to sit in their own section. Many times female abolitionists were not treated as equals to male abolitionists. Black female abolitionists faced the most obstacles to equal treatment.

Danger Ahead

Arguments between abolitionists and proslavery literature were the least of authors' problems. Writing a slave narrative could be dangerous. Frederick Douglass had to leave America after publishing his book. Because he had disclosed so many details about his life as a free man, Douglass's master came looking for him. Douglass then spent some time traveling abroad until his friends in England bought his freedom.

Frederick Douglass wasn't the only author on the run. James Norcom published a wanted ad in a Virginia newspaper looking for information about Harriet Jacobs after she escaped. The ad read as follows:

$100 REWARD

WILL be given for the apprehension and delivery of my Servant Girl HARRIET. She is a light mulatto, 21 years of age, about 5 feet 4 inches high, of a thick and corpulent habit, having on her head a thick covering of black hair that curls naturally, but which can be easily combed straight. She speaks easily and fluently, and has an agreeable carriage and address. Being a good seamstress, she has been accustomed to dress well, has a variety of very fine clothes, made in the prevailing fashion, and will probably appear, if abroad, tricked out in gay and fashionable finery. As this girl absconded from the plantation of my son without any known cause or provocation, it is probable she designs to transport herself to the North.

The above reward, with all reasonable charges, will be given for apprehending her, or securing her in any prison or jail within the U. States.

All persons are hereby forewarned against harboring or entertaining her, or being in any way instrumental in her escape, under the most rigorous penalties of the law.

JAMES NORCOM.

Edenton, N. C. June 30   372w

James Norcom placed this wanted ad offering a reward for Harriet Jacobs's capture.

In this ad, Norcom gives details about Jacobs's appearance. He also talks about her personality, what she might be wearing, and her plans. Norcom also promises that the $100 reward will be given to anyone who returns Jacobs or puts her in jail.

Former slaves knew the dangers of telling their stories. That is the reason many slave narratives leave out certain information. Authors might change the names of people and places. They did this to protect themselves and the people who helped them. Many slave narratives also use fake names for the people they describe. Leaving out information and using fake names were techniques that protected others and prevented a former slave's capture. Unfortunately, these techniques often raised suspicions about the truth of the stories.

People all over the North and South had strong feelings about slave narratives. They knew that these narratives were a big part of the abolitionist movement. People wrote good and bad reviews, created anti-Tom literature, and campaigned for and against slave narratives. Authors of slave narratives had to be careful after the Fugitive Slave Act passed. They changed details of their stories and even left the country—all to stay safe.

CHAPTER FOUR

The Legacy of Slave Narratives

S lave narratives, combined with speeches presented by their writers, led to the success of the abolitionist movement. Many people had never considered the lives of slaves. Then they read stories that showed that slaves were people, not objects to be bought and sold. More and more Americans began to understand that slavery was wrong. When they read about Uncle Tom being whipped or Harriet Jacobs hiding in a crawl space, they sympathized. They thought about their families and how life for them would be like if they were suddenly separated from their loved ones.

Abolitionists believed that all slaves should be free and worked hard to achieve this goal. Slave narratives were a big part of this campaign. They helped abolitionists convince others of the evils of slavery. Yet it's difficult

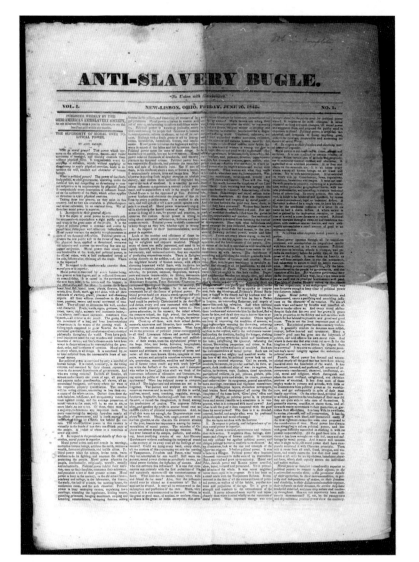

Anti-Slavery Bugle was an abolitionist newspaper. It included reports about abolitionist meetings, reviews of books, and editorials. Printing newspapers was just one way abolitionists worked toward ending slavery.

to say just how important slave narratives were to the success of abolitionism. There are too many factors.

Slave narratives were just one instrument in the abolitionist toolbox. Abolitionists started their own newspapers, wrote pamphlets, and held meetings to campaign for their cause. They helped slaves escape through the **Underground Railroad,** which was a network of houses where fugitive slaves could hide. Many slave narratives mention the Underground Railroad.

People's views about slavery changed over time without the influence of abolitionists, too. Even though it's impossible to tell their exact impact, slave narratives are the most lasting records of the people for whom abolitionists were fighting.

Slave Narratives and Emancipation

Sometimes people attending an abolitionist meeting had never met a former slave. They got to hear their stories firsthand and ask questions. In person it was difficult to deny the intelligence of Frederick Douglass or the passion of Sojourner Truth.

A man named John L. Lord attended an abolitionist meeting where William and Ellen Craft spoke. He wrote about the experience in a letter that was published in the *Liberator*.

> They held a meeting in the Court Street meeting-house ... which was filled to its utmost capacity—eight or nine hundred persons being present. A great many were unable to obtain admittance ... Mrs. Craft was then introduced to the audience, and gave a very particular account of their escape ... Friend Brown made a few more remarks, after which a collection was taken up.

Abolitionists started The American Anti-Slavery Society in 1833. This photograph shows the Philadelphia chapter's executive committee. Abolitionist groups had to be organized in order to plan meetings and activities for the cause.

> The audience then dispersed after a few anti-slavery songs by Mr. Brown, highly gratified with what they had heard and seen.

In this excerpt, Lord tells us that abolitionist meetings could be very large gatherings. Eight to nine hundred people listened to William and Ellen Craft speak at one meeting. He also talks about collecting donations, which allowed the Crafts and other abolitionist speakers to tour. He tells us the audience was "highly gratified," which means that they were pleased with what they had learned.

Escaped slaves and freedmen sold their slave narratives and gave speeches at abolitionist meetings for a few reasons:

- They wanted to help the abolitionist cause.
- Authors supported themselves using the money they earned from selling books.
- Earnings could be used to buy the freedom of friends and family left behind.

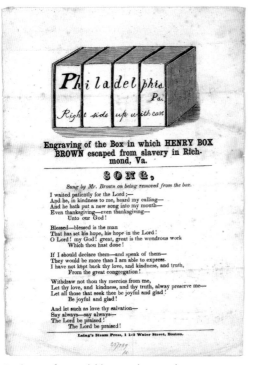

Engraving of the Box in which **HENRY BOX BROWN** escaped from slavery in Richmond, Va.

SONG,

Sung by Mr. Brown on being removed from the box.

I waited patiently for the Lord ;—
And he, in kindness to me, heard my calling—
And he hath put a new song into my mouth—
Even thanksgiving—even thanksgiving—
    Unto our God !

Blessed—blessed is the man
That has set his hope, his hope in the Lord !
O Lord ! my God ! great, great is the wondrous work
    Which thou hast done !

If I should declare them—and speak of them—
They would be more than I am able to express.
I have not kept back thy love, and kindness, and truth,
    From the great congregation !

Withdraw not thou thy mercies from me,
Let thy love, and kindness, and thy truth, alway preserve me—
Let all those that seek thee be joyful and glad !
    Be joyful and glad !

And let such as love thy salvation—
Say always—say always—
The Lord be praised !
    The Lord be praised !

Laing's Steam Press, 1 1-2 Water Street, Boston.

Authors often sold keepsakes such as engravings to promote their narratives and raise money.

Sojourner Truth worked her whole life to fight for causes in which she believed—including the abolitionist cause. She relied on the money she fundraised to continue her speaking tours. Truth often sold pictures of herself at speeches to raise money. She also received donations from other abolitionists.

The Anti Slavery Standard published a letter in 1863 that was written by Phebe Stickney, a friend of Truth's. In the letter, Truth thanked the supporters who provided her with donations.

As we opened the letters, one by one, and read the words of sweet remembrance and kindness, she was quite overcome with joy,

and more than once gave utterance to her
feelings through tears; praising the Lord
who had so soon answered her prayer,
which was, in language from the depths
of her soul, as she sat weary and alone in
her quiet little home: "Lord, I'm too old
to work—I'm too sick to hold meetings
and speak to de people, and sell my books;
Lord, you sent de ravens to feed 'Lijah in de
wilderness; now send de good angels to feed
me while I live on my footstool."

Sojourner Truth relied on her friends to write letters
for her because she could not write. Like many authors
of slave narratives, Truth made her living selling books
and giving lectures. When she could no longer do those
things, abolitionists sent money to help support her.

Authors worked for many years to end slavery.
Their slave narratives helped guide the nation toward
emancipation, or complete freedom, for all slaves. Slave
narratives helped northerners understand what the
institution of slavery was really like. The stories of escaped
and freed slaves helped to convince the North that slavery
was worth fighting against. When the Civil War started,
Abraham Lincoln promised that the aim of the war was
to keep the country together. The Southern states were
trying to form their own country to preserve slavery. As
the war continued, the goal changed. Lincoln decided to
work to end slavery. Slave narratives played a part in this
decision. When Abraham Lincoln met Harriet Beecher
Stowe in 1862, he supposedly said, "So you're the little

woman who wrote the book that started this great war." Even though Lincoln wasn't serious, his joke confirms that slave narratives played a part in ending slavery.

A Lasting Impact

Today we have access to thousands of slave narratives. This wasn't always the case. Many slave narratives went out of print after the Civil War. They had been an important part of the abolitionist movement, but people lost interest soon after slaves had been emancipated. Even the most famous slave narrative, *Narrative of the Life of Frederick Douglass*, disappeared from bookstores.

The Civil Rights movement brought new interest in slave narratives. In the 1950s and 1960s, African Americans were fighting for equal rights. Their fight included looking back in history and examining the past. Scholars began researching slave narratives and republishing stories. Researchers looked through primary sources such as letters, newspaper articles, and legal documents to prove that the details of many slave narratives were true.

Today Howard University, Fisk University, and the New York Public Library have large collections of slave narratives. Primary sources are available on the Internet, including abolitionist newspapers like the *Liberator*. The biggest collection of slave narratives is at the Library of Congress. In the 1930s, the government hired people to record the stories of former slaves. The collection contains more than 2,300 firsthand accounts, and all are available online. This group of narratives is called the Works Progress Administration (WPA) Slave Narratives.

Abraham Lincoln began the process of ending slavery when he issued the Emancipation Proclamation in 1863. Slave narratives helped shift public opinion toward emancipation.

The former slaves interviewed for the collection were getting very old. Some people question the accuracy of their memories. Others wonder if the interview subjects did not tell the whole truth because white men usually interviewed them. However, the WPA Slave Narratives are a great resource. These are narratives of former slaves who might not have been able to tell their stories otherwise. They are everyday people with their own unique experience of slavery. A former slave named Maggie Stenhouse was interviewed for the project. In her

WPA narrative she talked about events that took place after the Civil War.

> The Yankees rode three years over the country in squads and colored folks didn't know they was free. I have seen them in their old uniforms riding around when I was a child. White folks started talking about freedom for the darkies and turning them loose with the clothes they had on and what they could tote away. No land, no home, no place; they roamed around.

In this narrative Maggie speaks about the uncertain time after slaves were freed. It took a long time for the nation to rebuild. During this time, former slaves continued to write slave narratives. Booker T. Washington's *Up From Slavery* was the last slave narrative to be published. It was published in 1901.

Scholars today look at slave narratives in two ways: Slave narratives are studied as literature. They are also studied as important historical documents.

Slave Narratives as Literature

Slave narratives were forgotten for many years, but now literary critics recognize that narratives are pieces of literature. Literary critics are scholars who study important pieces of writing. Some of these scholars have written about how slave narratives fit into literature as a whole. Their research proves that slave narratives still influence writers today.

Slave narratives are the first pieces of African-American literature. Before slavery there were no African Americans, so slave narratives are the work of the earliest African-American writers. The authors of slave narratives have shaped the autobiographies of later writers. For example, scholars compare the writings of Malcolm X and Maya Angelou to slave narratives.

Maya Angelou's work was influenced by the genre of slave narratives.

Slave narratives have influenced fiction writers of all backgrounds. Herman Melville, William Styron, and Toni Morrison are just a few writers who have been inspired by the stories in slave narratives. Herman Melville lived in the 1800s, but Toni Morrison and William Styron are modern writers. Slave narratives have a wide influence. As literature they helped writers of all backgrounds and time periods to develop interesting stories.

Slave Narratives as Historical Documents

Slave narratives also changed the way we study the history of slavery. For many years, African-American studies began with the Emancipation Proclamation. Students did not learn about the experiences of slaves. They learned about what slavery was like for slave owners instead. Slave narratives convinced readers in the 1800s that slaves were people with rich experiences.

Sojourner Truth and "Ain't I a Woman?"

Sojourner Truth's "Ain't I a Woman?" speech is a great example of abolitionist writing that contains factual errors. Historians have studied the speech over the years. Using facts about Truth's life, they've determined that she probably never said the words "Ain't I a Woman?" Truth gave the speech off the top of her head. She never wrote it down because she could not write. The first written record of the speech was published a month after Truth delivered it.

Frances Dana Gage published the most famous version of the speech in 1863. Sojourner Truth had delivered the speech twelve years earlier. Truth grew up speaking Dutch. She lived in the North, so she wouldn't have spoken like a Southern woman. Yet Gage's version of "Ain't I a Woman?" includes many Southern pronunciations and phrases, including "ain't." Gage's record of the speech mentions Sojourner's "thirteen children," but Sojourner Truth had only five children. The mistakes in the speech show why it's important to question sources. The best historians use many primary sources to confirm facts.

Slave narratives had to convince people all over again in more recent times.

Historians examine slave narratives to learn details about the everyday lives of slaves. Slave narratives can tell us a lot about what slaves ate, wore, where they slept, what they learned, and what kind of work they did.

They also tell us the ways that slaves resisted slavery. Historians also help us understand which parts of slave narratives are factually incorrect.

Slave narratives have played many roles throughout history. They started as tools in the fight against slavery. Now they are studied as historical documents and loved as pieces of literature. The stories of Harriet Jacobs, Frederick Douglass, William and Ellen Craft, and Henry "Box" Brown contain daring escapes.

"AM I NOT A MAN AND A BROTHER?"

Abolitionists worked tirelessly to remind others that every person deserves freedom.

Sojourner Truth's speeches help us understand how the abolitionist movement grew and changed. Harriet Beecher Stowe committed to proving slavery was even worse than it was in her fictional story. But these are just a few authors of slave narratives. Thousands are available to us today. These narratives are the stories of everyday people living in horrible and inhumane conditions. They are stories of hope. They are stories of triumph.

Chronology

Dates in green pertain to events discussed in this volume.

1619 The African slave trade begins in North America.

1705 The first slave narratives are published.

1745 Olaudah Equiano is born in Nigeria.

1789 The US Constitution goes into effect.

1777–1804 Slavery is abolished in the northern states.

1789 *The Interesting Narrative of the Life of Olaudah Equiano, or Gustavo Vassa, the African* is published in London.

1808 The foreign slave trade is abolished by Great Britain and the United States.

1813 Harriet Jacobs is born in North Carolina.

1815 Henry "Box" Brown is born in Virginia.

1818 Frederick Douglass is born in Maryland.

1829 David Walker publishes *An Appeal to the Colored Citizens of the World*; states begin to make laws that prohibit teaching slaves to read or write.

1830–1860 The Underground Railroad helps about 50,000 slaves reach freedom.

1833 American Anti-Slavery Society is founded in Philadelphia.

1837–1839 The Grimké sisters speak against slavery to overflow audiences in New York and New England.

1845 Frederick Douglass publishes *Narrative of the Life of Frederick Douglass, an American Slave*.

1848 William and Ellen Craft travel from Georgia to Pennsylvania to become free.

1849 Harriet Tubman escapes from slavery into Pennsylvania; James W. C. Pennington publishes *The Fugitive Blacksmith*; Henry "Box" Brown escapes to the north by mailing himself in a box from Virginia to Pennsylvania.

1850 The US Congress passes the Fugitive Slave Act; slave narratives become best sellers.

1851 *Uncle Tom's Cabin* runs as a serial in the abolitionist newspaper *National Era* in Washington, DC; Sojourner Truth gives her speech titled "Ain't I a Woman?" in Akron, Ohio.

1852 Stowe's complete novel, *Uncle Tom's Cabin*, sells millions of copies.

1854 Congress approves the Kansas-Nebraska Act.

1855–1860 Harriet Tubman rescues freedom seekers and leads them from Maryland to Canada.

1856 Proslavery activists attack the antislavery town of Lawrence, Kansas; John Brown leads a raid on a proslavery family, which launches a three-month conflict known as "Bleeding Kansas."

1857 The Supreme Court hands down its decision in the *Dred Scott v Sanford* case.

1859 John Brown launches an attack at Harpers Ferry.

1860 Abraham Lincoln is elected president; South Carolina secedes from the Union.

1861 The Civil War begins; Harriet Jacobs publishes *Incidents in the Life of a Slave Girl, Written by Herself.*

1863 Lincoln's Emancipation Proclamation frees the slaves in Confederate-held territory.

1865 The Civil War ends. President Lincoln is assassinated. The Thirteenth Amendment to the US Constitution abolishes slavery.

1866 The American Equal Rights Association is formed. Its goals are to establish equal rights and the vote for women and African Americans.

1868 The Fourteenth Amendment grants US citizenship to former slaves.

1870 The Fifteenth Amendment gives black men the right to vote.

1896 A group of black civil rights activists form the National Association of Colored Women in Washington, DC. The group works to further civil rights for blacks and obtain the vote for women.

Glossary

abolish To end something, usually by passing a law.

abolitionist A person working to end slavery because they believe slavery is wrong.

anti-Tom literature Nineteenth-century proslavery novels and other literary works written in response to Harriet Beecher Stowe's *Uncle Tom's Cabin*.

big house The house in which a slave owner lived with his family.

court To date; to engage in social activities leading to engagement and marriage.

emancipation Legal freedom from slavery.

fugitive A person who runs away from an enemy, a master, duty, or the law.

Fugitive Slave Act A law passed in 1850 that made it a crime to help runaway slaves.

master Another name for a slave owner; what slaves called the person who owned them.

mulatto A person of mixed white and black ancestry; usually offensive.

narrative A story with a beginning, middle, and end.

peculiar institution Another name for slavery.

plantation A farm in the South where slaves lived and worked.

poultice Medicine worn under a piece of cloth.

segregated Separated by race.

slave catcher Someone who looked for fugitive slaves hoping to collect a reward.

slaveholder Another name for a slave owner.

slave quarters Small cabins in which slave families lived on a plantation.

Underground Railroad A network of abolitionists who cooperated in helping slaves along their way to freedom in the North or Canada.

Further Information

Books

Erickson, Paul. *Daily Life on a Southern Plantation, 1853*. New York: Lodestar Books, 1998.

Freedman, Florence B., and Ezra Jack Keats. *Two Tickets to Freedom: The True Story of Ellen and William Craft, Fugitive Slaves*. New York: Simon and Schuster, 1971.

Hamilton, Virginia, Leo Dillon, and Diane Dillon. *Many Thousand Gone: African Americans from Slavery to Freedom*. New York: Knopf, 1993.

Lester, Julius, and Tom Feelings. *To Be a Slave*. New York: Dial Press, 1968.

Levin, Judith. *A Timeline of the Abolitionist Movement*. New York: Rosen Central, 2004.

Websites

America's Library

www.americaslibrary.gov

Explore the timeline of events in the "Westward Expansion and Reform" section to read more about abolitionists and African-American historical figures.

OurStory

www.amhistory.si.edu/ourstory

The Smithsonian Institute's OurStory has activities, book suggestions, and field trip ideas. Take part in a virtual archaeological exploration and discover objects used in the religious rites and spiritual practices of slaves.

The Slave Experience

www.pbs.org/wnet/slavery

Browse various topics about slave life, such as religion, living conditions, and legal rights. Each section includes an overview, primary sources, and biographies.

Bibliography

"Ain't I A Woman?" Sojourner Truth Institute. Accessed November 9, 2014. www.sojournertruth.org/Library /Speeches/AintIAWoman.htm.

Andrews, William L. *North Carolina Slave Narratives: The Lives of Moses Roper, Lunsford Lane, and Moses Grandy & Thomas H. Jones*. Chapel Hill, NC: University of North Carolina Press, 2003.

Andrews, William L., ed. *Six Women's Slave Narratives*. New York: Oxford University Press, 1988.

"A Report on Speeches Made by William Wells Brown and William and Ellen Craft, 1849." Documenting the American South. Accessed November 9, 2014. www.docsouth.unc.edu/neh/craft/support2.html.

Bontemps, Arna, ed. *Great Slave Narratives*. Boston: Beacon Press, 1969.

"Born in Slavery: Slave Narratives from the Federal Writers' Project, 1936-1938." Library of Congress. Accessed November 10, 2014. www.memory.loc.gov /ammem/snhtml/.

Brown, Henry Box. *Narrative of the Life of Henry Box Brown*. New York: Oxford University Press, 2002.

Douglass, Frederick. *Narrative of the Life of Frederick Douglass*. New York: Dover Publications, 1995.

"GRASSHOPPERS." *The Sun*, August 6, 1859.

"Incidents in the Life of a Slave Girl; the Narrative of Linda Brent." *Anti-Slavery Bugle*, February 9, 1861.

Jacobs, Harriet A., and Lydia Maria Child. *Incidents in the Life of a Slave Girl, Written by Herself*. Cambridge, MA: Harvard University Press, 1987.

Katz, William, ed. *Five Slave Narratives: A Compendium*. New York: Arno Press, 1968.

Kolchin, Peter. *American Slavery, 1619–1877*. New York: Hill and Wang, 1993.

Sorin, Gerald. *Abolitionism: A New Perspective*. New York: Praeger, 1972.

Stowe, Harriet Beecher. *The Key to Uncle Tom's Cabin*. New York: Arno Press, 1968.

Stowe, Harriet Beecher. *Uncle Tom's Cabin, Or, Life among the Lowly*. New York: Modern Library, 2001.

White, Deborah G. *Ar'n't I a Woman?: Female Slaves in the Plantation South*. New York: Norton, 1999.

Yee, Shirley J. *Black Women Abolitionists: A Study in Activism, 1828–1860*. Knoxville: University of Tennessee Press, 1992.

Index

Page numbers in **boldface** are illustrations. Entries in **boldface** are glossary terms.

About the Author

CAITLYN PALEY lives on the Eastern Shore of Maryland near the birthplace of Frederick Douglass. She enjoys history and poetry, so she was excited to learn about the slave poet Phillis Wheatley while researching this book. Paley also likes to run, hike, eat cake, and take road trips.

H5